JUDI DENCH

A BIOGRAPHY

A Life in Theatre, Film, and Television

Paradise Report

Table of contents

Brief history of Dame Judi Dench

Judi Dench's formative years were characterised by an abiding passion for the theatrical arts. Having spent her formative years in the charming city of York, England, she was fortunate enough to be immersed in the world of arts from an early age. It was during her time in school that her innate talent for performing became unmistakably apparent, as she eagerly took part in various theatrical productions. Following the successful completion of her education, Dench diligently pursued her aspirations and took the decisive step of enrolling at the esteemed Central School of Speech and Drama in London. This event signified the commencement of her formal education, establishing the groundwork for her remarkable and distinguished professional trajectory.

Upon completing her studies at drama school, Dench swiftly embarked on a journey to establish her presence in the realm of theatre. With her remarkable prowess in the craft of acting and her remarkable ability to adapt to various roles, she embarked on a journey that would lead her to become a member of the esteemed Royal Shakespeare Company in 1961, leaving an enduring legacy in the process. The actress's portrayal in renowned Shakespearean plays such as "Hamlet," "King Lear," and "Antony and Cleopatra" served to firmly establish her standing as an exceptional performer on the theatrical stage.

Dame Judi Dench, a multifaceted artist, demonstrated her versatility by venturing beyond the confines of the stage. Throughout the 1970s, she gradually broadened her footprint in the realms of film and television. In 1985, she achieved a significant milestone in her career by securing her inaugural BAFTA Award for her exceptional portrayal in the renowned cinematic masterpiece, "A Room with a View." The acknowledgment bestowed upon me has served as a catalyst for an array of new prospects within the realm of the cinematic arts.

In the year 1997, Dame Judi Dench's illustrious career soared to unprecedented heights as she garnered the prestigious accolade of an Academy Award. This esteemed recognition was bestowed upon her for her remarkable portrayal of the iconic Queen Elizabeth I in the critically acclaimed film "Shakespeare in Love." This notable accomplishment served to further establish her standing as an esteemed actress, while also earning her widespread recognition on a global scale. Her name became indelibly linked with the concept of excellence, and her unparalleled talent for embodying characters with profound complexity and subtlety enthralled audiences across the globe.

Throughout the subsequent years, Dench's luminosity persisted to radiate on the silver screen, effortlessly captivating audiences with her indelible portrayals in cinematic masterpieces such as "Mrs. Brown," "Chocolat," "Iris," and "Notes on a Scandal." With her remarkable talent for infusing humanity into her portrayals, be it of historical figures or fictional characters, she has garnered immense admiration from both filmmakers and audiences alike.

A Life Well Lived

As Dame Judi Dench embarked upon her octogenarian years, her unwavering dedication to her craft and steadfast commitment to utilising her influence for the betterment of society remained resolute. With unwavering dedication, she persistently engaged in a multitude of projects spanning the realms of film, television, and theatre, thereby showcasing her inexhaustible ardour for the craft of acting. In addition to her illustrious career on both stage and screen, Dench has dedicated a significant portion of her time to philanthropic endeavours. She has graciously assumed the role of patron for numerous organisations, lending her support and influence to their causes. Furthermore, Dench has emerged as a vocal champion for women's rights, fearlessly advocating for gender equality and empowerment.

The life of Judi Dench stands as a testament to the profound influence that can be achieved through diligent effort, resolute determination, and unwavering commitment to one's true calling. The trajectory of her path, beginning as an aspiring actress in York and culminating in her status as an international icon, serves as a wellspring of inspiration for both burgeoning artists and individuals seeking personal growth. The enduring legacy of her remarkable talent as an actress, her unwavering commitment as a role model, and her passionate advocacy will serve as a perpetual source of inspiration for future generations. Dame Judi Dench has undeniably led a life that is truly deserving of celebration and admiration.

Purpose of this book

The book's purpose is to provide a captivating celebration of an iconic figure.

"Judi Dench: Life in Theatre, Film, and Television is an enthralling tribute that commemorates the extraordinary life and illustrious career of Judi Dench, an actress of unparalleled talent and endearment, who has left an indelible mark on the world of performing arts. This literary work takes readers on a profound exploration of the different stages in her life, skillfully intertwining a vibrant tapestry that chronicles her ascent to stardom, individual victories, and remarkable odyssey as a female figure in the realm of entertainment.

The narrative commences by immersing itself in Judi Dench's modest origins in York, England, where her fervour for the theatrical arts was kindled. Immersing readers in a captivating narrative, they will be effortlessly transported to the pivotal moments that intricately shaped her formative years, ultimately serving as influential catalysts in her resolute determination to embark on a profound journey in the realm of acting. As she gracefully manoeuvres through the hallowed halls of the esteemed Central School of Speech and Drama in the vibrant city of London, a profound glimpse into her unwavering resolve and unwavering commitment to her craft emerges. It becomes abundantly clear that these qualities have propelled her towards an extraordinary destiny, one marked by unparalleled achievements and resounding success.

The narrative traces her journey as she ascended to fame, enchanting audiences with her stage performances and attaining a revered position within the esteemed Royal Shakespeare Company. The book vividly captures her indelible performances in iconic Shakespearean plays such as "Hamlet," "King Lear," and "Antony and Cleopatra," illuminating the profound range and adaptability that established her as a formidable presence in the realm of theatre.

However, this biography transcends the boundaries of a mere chronicle of accomplishments. This narrative delves deep into the intricate tapestry of Judi Dench's personal life, exploring the nuances of her relationships and the formidable challenges she encountered on her journey. Through the pages of this compelling narrative, readers will be granted a profound and intimate glimpse into the inner world of the woman who stands as an icon of the silver screen. As she traverses the intricate tapestry of love, grapples with the profound depths of loss, and tenaciously pursues her aspirations, her unwavering resilience serves as a beacon of inspiration.

At the core of this literary work resides its profound ability to ignite inspiration. As readers delve into the pages of this captivating narrative, they will bear witness to the remarkable journey of Judi Dench, a life that defies the boundaries of a conventional biography, propelling her to the esteemed position of an extraordinary exemplar. She embodies a symbol of optimism, demonstrating that remarkable achievements can be reached, even in the absence of advantageous circumstances. The tale of her triumph stands as a poignant testament to the fact that women have the capacity to thrive in their professional endeavours while simultaneously nurturing meaningful familial relationships.

Furthermore, "Judi Dench: A Life on Stage and Screen" exalts the exquisite art of gracefully embracing the passage of time. The narrative of her life exemplifies the myriad joys and challenges that accompany the progression of time, illuminating the profound capacity for individuals to embrace their personal odyssey with grace and fortitude, thereby perpetuating a meaningful influence even in the twilight of their existence.

With its vibrant and captivating prose, the book guarantees to hold readers enthralled from beginning to end. Within the pages of this literary masterpiece, one will discover a plethora of captivating anecdotes and profound insights that offer a glimpse into the extraordinary life of this iconic actress. The text is accompanied by stunning photographs that offer captivating visual insights into the pivotal moments that have shaped her remarkable career.

This biography is an essential literary work for individuals who hold a deep admiration for Judi Dench, as well as those who find themselves captivated by the enchanting realm of theatre and film. It stands as a testament to the formidable influence of diligent effort, unwavering commitment, and fervent enthusiasm. Significantly, it evokes a profound sense of inspiration among individuals from diverse backgrounds, as they glean invaluable lessons from an authentic legend on the art of resilience and leaving an indelible impact on the world. As one delves into the pages of this literary masterpiece, one must be prepared to experience a profound emotional journey, to be captivated by the indomitable spirit of Judi Dench, an enduring symbol of excellence whose narrative will undoubtedly leave an indelible mark on our collective consciousness, transcending time and inspiring future generations.

Introduction

The attainment of legendary status necessitates the harmonious convergence of inherent aptitude, resolute commitment, and a fortuitous twist of fate. Judi Dench personifies these qualities, and her path to attaining the status of one of the most esteemed and beloved actresses globally serves as a testament to her unwavering determination.

Since the inception of her career, Judi Dench exhibited an indisputable aptitude for the arts. The genesis of her affection for the theatre took root during her formative years in York, England. It was there that she immersed herself in school productions, diligently refining her skills and establishing the bedrock upon which her forthcoming triumphs would be built. Her choice to embark on a professional acting career propelled her towards the esteemed Central School of Speech and Drama in London, a renowned institution where she honed her skills and embarked on a journey towards achieving greatness.

Dench's resolute dedication to her craft led her to become a member of the esteemed Royal Shakespeare Company in 1961, where she wholeheartedly immersed herself in the realm of classical theatre. With unwavering determination, she triumphed over the formidable obstacles that the stage presented, ultimately earning herself a well-deserved reputation for her masterful interpretations of the timeless Shakespearean figures. During this pivotal phase of her career, she cemented her status as an extraordinary actress, garnering admiration and esteem from both her colleagues and discerning critics.

Making the leap from the theatrical stage to the illustrious silver screen, Dame Judi Dench encountered formidable obstacles in the shape of deeply ingrained sexism and ageism, which regrettably remain pervasive within the realm of entertainment. Instead of yielding to these challenges, she confronted them directly, displaying unwavering resolve and elegance. Through her steadfast commitment to her craft, she managed to surpass all expectations, thereby demonstrating that talent knows no boundaries of age or gender.

In the face of personal hardships, notably the tragic loss of her husband, Judi Dench exhibited unwavering determination, refusing to allow adversity to impede the pursuit of her dreams. Instead, she skillfully harnessed her emotions and personal experiences, seamlessly integrating them into her performances, imbuing her characters with profound depth and unwavering authenticity.

The turning point in her career materialised in 1997, as she emerged victorious in the esteemed Academy Awards, securing an Oscar for her remarkable portrayal of Queen Elizabeth I in the renowned film "Shakespeare in Love." The attainment of this esteemed accolade signified a pivotal moment in her professional trajectory, effectively highlighting her aptitude for making a profound impression on global audiences.

Over the course of her illustrious career, Dame Judi Dench's name became indelibly associated with a standard of excellence that few could rival. She consistently mesmerised audiences with her captivating performances in a plethora of critically acclaimed films, including notable titles such as "Mrs. Brown," "Chocolat," and numerous others. Through the embodiment of each distinct role, she effortlessly infused vitality into her characters, thereby etching an enduring imprint upon the annals of cinematic history.

The remarkable trajectory of Judi Dench's rise to legendary status stands as a timeless source of inspiration for aspiring actors and individuals hailing from diverse backgrounds. The unwavering dedication she exhibits in chasing her aspirations, combined with her unwavering determination to surmount obstacles, embodies the very essence of an authentic icon. Through her unwavering determination, unyielding spirit, and relentless pursuit of her goals, she exemplifies the profound truth that no matter the challenges that life presents, greatness can indeed be attained.

With her exceptional talent and remarkable achievements, she has not only garnered numerous accolades but also captured the hearts of countless admirers across the globe. As Judi Dench continues to captivate audiences on both stage and screen, she stands as a shining example of hope and a symbol of the extraordinary journey towards becoming a true legend. Her remarkable story serves as a testament to the profound influence that can be achieved by pursuing one's dreams with resolute determination and an indomitable spirit. Undoubtedly, her legacy will serve as a timeless inspiration for future generations, establishing her as an enduring icon within the realm of entertainment and a source of motivation for those who possess the audacity to pursue ambitious dreams.

Chapter 1: The Early Years
Childhood in York

Judi Dench's early years in York, England, laid the foundation for her extraordinary journey to becoming a legendary actress. Born on December 9, 1934, she grew up in a nurturing and loving middle-class family, with her father, Reginald Arthur Dench, serving as a doctor, and her mother, Eleanora Olive Jones, dedicating herself to creating a warm and supportive home.

Judi's childhood was enriched by the vibrant cultural offerings of her hometown, York. She attended a Quaker school, where she was instilled with values of compassion, simplicity, and community spirit. Although naturally shy, young

Judi discovered her passion for performing early on, finding solace and joy in the world of theatre.

Her fascination with the stage became evident as she participated in school plays, where her innate talent for emotive storytelling and captivating audiences became evident. Even at a young age, she displayed an unmistakable spark, drawing attention for her ability to transform into different characters with ease.

Inspired by her grandmother, a talented amateur actress, Judi Dench dreamt of following in her footsteps and making her mark in the world of theatre. This aspiration was nurtured by her family, who recognized and encouraged her burgeoning passion for the performing arts.

At the age of 16, her dreams took a significant step forward as she landed her first professional acting role at the renowned York Theatre Royal. Playing a small part in "The Taming of the Shrew," she felt the thrill of the spotlight and the magic of the stage, solidifying her conviction to pursue acting as a career.

However, her journey towards stardom was not without its challenges. Despite her undeniable talent and unwavering determination, Dench faced hurdles typical of the era, as opportunities for women in the arts were often limited and overshadowed by pervasive sexism. Undeterred, she pressed on, undeniably driven by her unwavering love for the craft.

As she graduated from school, Dench's dedication to her passion led her to the esteemed Central

School of Speech and Drama in London. This transformative period marked a crucial chapter in her life, shaping her skills, building her confidence, and preparing her to take on the world of professional acting.

The early years were formative for Judi Dench, as she laid the groundwork for her illustrious career. With each step, she gained invaluable experiences, developing her artistic sensibility and building the resilience that would serve her well in the face of future challenges.

In her childhood home of York, amidst the picturesque surroundings and rich cultural heritage, Judi Dench's journey as a true icon began. Her passion for the arts and unwavering determination to succeed painted the canvas of her future, destined to become a living legend in the world of entertainment.

A Love of Theatre

From a tender age, Judi Dench's deep connection to the world of theatre became an integral part of her very essence, laying the groundwork for a truly extraordinary career that would endure for more than six decades. The inception of her acting career was marked by a profound affection for the theatrical realm, which flourished into an unyielding commitment and propelled her to attain the status of a bona fide luminary within the realm of stagecraft.

Since her formative years, Dench was enthralled by the enchantment of the theatrical world. In the company of her loved ones, she partook in the experience of attending theatrical performances, and she was immediately captivated by the enchantment that unfolded before her very eyes. The performances of the actors, the narratives they conveyed, and the tangible emotions that permeated the atmosphere left an enduring mark on her youthful heart.

As Judi Dench matured, her ardour for the stage intensified, unveiling her inherent aptitude for the craft of acting. Her passion was nurtured by her grandmother, an amateur actress, who played a pivotal role in fueling this love. The encouragement of her grandmother, combined with the exposure to live performances, served as a catalyst, igniting a profound passion within her and compelling her to actively engage in school plays.

With the recognition of her innate talent and captivating stage presence, Dench's path towards a career in acting began to gather momentum. She embarked on her journey towards a promising acting career by enrolling at the renowned Central School of Speech and Drama in London. In that place, she refined her skills, immersing herself in the art with unwavering commitment that would prove invaluable in her professional journey.

Following her graduation in 1957, Judi Dench embarked on a remarkable professional acting career, venturing into a world that would ultimately propel her to the pinnacle of the theatre industry. Having collaborated with the renowned Old Vic Company and subsequently becoming a member of the esteemed Royal Shakespeare Company, she wholeheartedly embraced the realm of classical theatre. Through her exceptional portrayals of iconic characters, she delivered awe-inspiring performances that captivated audiences and left them utterly enthralled.

Despite achieving tremendous success in the realms of film and television, Judi Dench's unwavering passion for the theatre endured. The irresistible charm of the stage, the instantaneous rapport with the audience, and the exhilaration of live performances beckoned her repeatedly. She had previously articulated her profound affinity for theatre, as it provided her with an exceptional opportunity to delve into the intricacies of characters and emotions within an intimately immersive environment.

Throughout the years, Judi Dench has made remarkable contributions to the world of theatre that can only be described as extraordinary. Boasting an impressive repertoire of more than 100 theatrical productions, she has earned widespread acclaim for her remarkable range, consistently infusing each character she portrays with an unmatched sense of authenticity and profound emotional depth. The remarkable prowess she possesses has garnered widespread acclaim and has been duly honoured through a multitude of prestigious accolades, notably including two Olivier Awards and a highly esteemed Tony Award.

Judi Dench's remarkable contributions to the arts were duly recognized through her appointment as a Dame of the British Empire, a testament to the enduring influence she has had on the theatrical realm. In the year 2011, she was graciously bestowed with the prestigious Praemium Imperiale, a distinguished honour presented by the esteemed Japan Art Association. This accolade was in recognition of her profound and significant contributions to the realm of theatre, as well as her exceptional achievements as a highly accomplished actress.

Her enduring passion for the stage remains unwavering, and with every captivating performance, she consistently ignites inspiration within aspiring actors and theatre enthusiasts across the globe. Judi Dench's unwavering dedication to her craft, her profound passion, and her remarkable ability to deeply resonate with audiences epitomise the authentic essence of the theatrical art form. With a remarkable presence in the world of theatre and an esteemed reputation, she serves as a testament to the profound impact of art, leaving behind a lasting legacy that will undoubtedly ignite inspiration for future generations.

Her First Break

The year 1957 marked a significant milestone in the realm of theatre, as a remarkable young talent named Judi Dench, at the tender age of 22, achieved her breakthrough that would propel her into the realm of fame and recognition. Dame Judi Dench, a distinguished member of the esteemed Old Vic Company, was bestowed with the pivotal role of Ophelia in a production of "Hamlet." This character portrayal served as a significant milestone in her journey towards establishing herself as a revered figure in the realm of theatre.

The portrayal of Ophelia by the artist was truly exceptional, garnering high praise from both critics and spectators. Dench's portrayal of the tragic character emanated a profound depth and emotional intensity that surpassed her years, leaving an indelible impression on all fortunate enough to witness her performance on the stage. The critics, in particular, bestowed upon her the accolade of being "a star in the making," acknowledging the profound reservoir of talent that resided within her.

The pivotal role Dench played in "Hamlet" served as a catalyst for her rapidly developing career. With her undeniable talent and commanding presence, she swiftly garnered additional opportunities on the stage, thereby solidifying her standing as one of the most promising young actresses of her generation. Her remarkable talent for fully immersing herself in every character she portrayed left audiences captivated. With an unparalleled authenticity, she brought classic plays to life in a way that was truly spellbinding and awe-inspiring.

The trajectory of Judi Dench's career ascended further as she embarked upon a new phase in her theatrical odyssey in 1961, when she became a member of the esteemed Royal Shakespeare Company (RSC). This pivotal moment in her career signified yet another noteworthy milestone, affording her the opportunity to collaborate with esteemed luminaries within the industry and showcase her talents in a multitude of Shakespeare's legendary theatrical productions. Dame Judi Dench's remarkable range and talent were prominently showcased through her portrayal of multifaceted characters such as Lady Macbeth, Desdemona in "Othello," and the astute Portia in "The Merchant of Venice." Her ability to seamlessly embody these diverse roles captivated audiences, leaving them spellbound by her every nuanced performance.

Alongside her notable performances in Shakespearean plays, Dench ventured into other renowned works such as "Oedipus Rex" and "The Cherry Orchard," thereby cementing her standing as a formidable actress renowned for her adeptness in portraying a wide array of characters with finesse.

The initial breakthrough in Judi Dench's career not only granted her opportunities as an actress but also established the foundation for a lasting legacy that transcended the boundaries of the theatrical realm. With an unwavering commitment to her craft, she consistently showcased her exceptional talent, earning her a multitude of accolades. Throughout her illustrious career, she was honoured with several prestigious awards, including two Olivier Awards and a Tony Award.

The occurrence of this groundbreaking moment marked a significant milestone that propelled Judi Dench to the upper echelons of British acting. The platform provided her with an opportunity to display her exceptional talents to a broader audience, garnering the esteem and admiration of both her colleagues and avid theatre enthusiasts. As her career continued to thrive, Dench's star radiated with increasing brilliance, leaving an enduring imprint on the realm of entertainment and solidifying her position as one of the most revered and adored actresses in history.

The initial breakthrough experienced by Judi Dench was not merely an opportunity, but rather a catalyst that ignited a remarkable career extending over a span of more than six decades. With an unwavering commitment to her craft and an undeniable ardour for the stage, she embarked on a path that would ultimately catapult her to the pinnacle of success, solidifying her status as a revered figure in the realm of theatre and a beacon of motivation for budding thespians worldwide.

Chapter 2: The Rise to Fame

The ascent of Judi Dench to stardom can only be described as a truly extraordinary odyssey, characterised by her indomitable spirit, exceptional aptitude, and relentless pursuit of her aspirations. In the face of numerous challenges, she ascended to greatness, leaving an enduring imprint on the realm of entertainment and emerging as a genuine icon in the hearts of countless individuals.

At the young age of 16, she experienced her initial foray into the realm of professional acting, obtaining a modest role in the esteemed production of "The Taming of the Shrew" at the renowned York Theatre Royal. The initial encounter sparked a profound passion within her, leading her to the realisation that the stage was her rightful place. The commencement of her journey towards her aspirations laid the foundation for a forthcoming replete with resplendent achievements in the realm of theatre.

Following her rigorous training at the renowned Central School of Speech and Drama in London, Dench embarked on a notable journey by becoming a member of the esteemed Old Vic Company. Having dedicated multiple years to her tenure with the company, she assumed illustrious characters in timeless theatrical productions such as "Hamlet," "King Lear," and "Antony and Cleopatra." With an undeniable magnetic stage presence and an exceptional display of talent, she swiftly captured the attention of audiences, solidifying her position as a prominent actress within her generation.

In the year 1961, a significant turning point unfolded in her professional journey as she became a member of the esteemed Royal Shakespeare Company (RSC), widely regarded as one of the foremost theatre companies on a global scale. Immersed in the works of Shakespeare, she wholeheartedly delved into her portrayal of iconic characters like Lady Macbeth, Desdemona, and Portia in the renowned play "The Merchant of Venice." Her performances were nothing short of brilliant. Dench's performances were widely acclaimed for their profound depth and unwavering authenticity, eliciting admiration from both discerning critics and captivated audiences.

Although theatre continued to be her primary passion, Dench's talent began to transcend the boundaries of the stage. During the 1970s, she embarked upon a foray into the realm of film and television, effectively demonstrating her remarkable range and exceptional acting abilities within this novel artistic domain. The manner in which she depicted characters on the screen was equally captivating, resulting in her receiving commendations and amassing a burgeoning group of devoted admirers.

During her ascent to stardom, Dench encountered significant obstacles. She courageously confronted the pervasive issues of sexism and ageism within the entertainment industry, demonstrating unwavering determination in the face of these formidable obstacles. With unwavering determination and an indomitable spirit, she forged ahead, demonstrating that a combination of innate ability, unwavering resolve, and inner fortitude has the power to surmount any challenge.

In the year 1985, her exceptional portrayal in the film "A Room with a View" garnered her the highly esteemed BAFTA Award, marking the commencement of a remarkably fruitful trajectory in the world of cinema. The acknowledgment she received expanded her reach, solidifying her position as a formidable presence in the realm of film.

In 1997, a significant milestone in her distinguished career was reached as she was bestowed with an Academy Award for her remarkable depiction of Queen Elizabeth I in the renowned film "Shakespeare in Love." Her triumph at the Oscars cemented her position as a revered luminary, elevating her to the esteemed ranks of a worldwide icon within the realm of cinema.

Nevertheless, amidst her meteoric ascent to stardom, Dench was confronted with profound personal tragedy. In the year 1995, her spouse and esteemed colleague in the acting profession, Michael Williams, succumbed to the perils of cancer, resulting in an overwhelming sense of devastation for her. Confronted with this profound loss, she sought solace in her work, utilising her craft as a means to find healing and navigate the depths of grief.

The ascent of Judi Dench to stardom stands as a remarkable testament to her exceptional talent, unwavering determination, and remarkable poise. With an unwavering commitment to her craft and a remarkable talent for forging deep connections with audiences, she has undeniably established herself as an iconic figure in the realm of entertainment.

With an impressive array of accomplishments, she has garnered numerous accolades throughout her illustrious career. Notably, she has received two additional BAFTA Awards for her exceptional performances in "Chocolat" (2000) and "Iris" (2001). Her remarkable contributions to the arts have been recognized with esteemed honours such as her Damehood in 1988, the prestigious Kennedy Center Honor in 2007, and the esteemed Praemium Imperiale in 2011. These accolades serve as a testament to the profound and lasting impact she has made in the realm of artistic expression.

The ascent of Judi Dench to stardom stands as a testament to her remarkable odyssey, commencing as a young girl enthralled by the enchantment of the theatre and culminating in her esteemed status as an internationally admired actress. Her story serves as an inspiration to women across the globe, standing as a testament to the immense influence of talent, unwavering perseverance, and the relentless pursuit of one's aspirations. The enduring legacy of her iconic status will serve as a timeless source of inspiration for future generations, guaranteeing that her luminous presence will forever remain indelible within the realm of entertainment.

The Royal Shakespeare Company (RSC) is a renowned theatrical organisation that has established itself as a prominent force in the world of performing arts. With a rich history spanning several decades, the RSC has consistently delivered exceptional productions of The Royal Shakespeare Company (RSC) is widely regarded as a prestigious institution within the realm of theatre. It captivates audiences and aspiring actors alike through its innovative productions and unwavering dedication to upholding the legacy of William Shakespeare's literary masterpieces.

The Royal Shakespeare Company (RSC) was established in 1961 by esteemed individuals Peter Hall, Peter Brook, and John Barton. Their collective vision was to present the works of Shakespeare in a manner that would be more readily accessible and captivating to audiences. In a departure from the customary, intricate period attire, the Royal Shakespeare Company (RSC) embraced a contemporary approach to costuming, imbuing Shakespeare's enduring narratives with a modern sensibility that struck a chord with diverse audiences. In addition, they engaged in the exploration of avant-garde staging techniques, thereby infusing the timeless classics with a renewed vitality.

Ever since its establishment, the Royal Shakespeare Company (RSC) has experienced a remarkable ascent, garnering widespread acclaim and establishing itself as a preeminent theatrical organisation on a global scale. It has earned a well-deserved reputation as one of the largest and most esteemed companies in the realm of theatre. With an extensive repertoire boasting more than 300 productions of Shakespeare's plays, alongside a collection of works crafted by other esteemed playwrights, their artistic portfolio stands as a testament to their profound dedication to the theatrical arts.

The Royal Shakespeare Company (RSC) has garnered widespread acclaim, receiving numerous prestigious accolades such as Olivier Awards, Tony Awards, and Grammy Awards. These esteemed honours serve as a testament to the RSC's unwavering commitment to pushing boundaries and setting new standards in the realm of theatrical brilliance.

Significantly, the Royal Shakespeare Company (RSC) transcends the conventional boundaries of a mere theatre company, as it serves as a fertile breeding ground for burgeoning talents. The Academy of the Royal Shakespeare Company provides extensive training programs tailored to actors, directors, designers, and technicians, offering a valuable platform for emerging artists to hone their craft and cultivate their artistic abilities.

Alongside its unwavering dedication to theatrical tradition, the Royal Shakespeare Company (RSC) has consistently demonstrated its pioneering spirit by seamlessly integrating new technologies into their productions. The individuals in question were trailblazers in the utilisation of video projections to elevate the visual encounter for spectators. Moreover, they have ventured into the realm of state-of-the-art technologies, including virtual reality and augmented reality, in order to expand the horizons of narrative expression.

The Royal Shakespeare Company (RSC) has a rich and storied past, marked by a multitude of remarkable productions that have made an indelible mark on the realms of theatre and popular culture. Among the most remarkable theatrical achievements, one cannot overlook Peter O'Toole's masterful depiction of "Hamlet" in the year 1964. Equally captivating was Judi Dench's unforgettable portrayal in "A Midsummer Night's Dream" during the year 1970. Ian McKellen's mesmerising interpretation of "The Tempest" in 1974 left audiences spellbound, while Derek Jacobi's commanding rendition of "King Lear" in 1986 left an indelible impact. Lastly, Ian McKellen's chilling performance as "Richard III" in 1995 remains etched in the memories of those fortunate enough to witness it.

The Royal Shakespeare Company's unwavering dedication to ensuring the accessibility of Shakespeare's plays to a wide range of audiences, coupled with its steadfast commitment to fostering the growth of emerging talents, has firmly established it as an indispensable cultural institution within the United Kingdom. The enduring ability to inspire and captivate theatre enthusiasts persists, as it guarantees that the timeless words of Shakespeare reverberate within the hearts of new generations.

The enduring impact of the Royal Shakespeare Company is rooted in its rich tradition of innovation, unwavering commitment to artistic excellence, and steadfast preservation of the timeless essence of classical theatre. This legacy guarantees that its profound influence will reverberate throughout the cultural landscape of the United Kingdom and extend far beyond, resonating with future generations for years to come. The Royal Shakespeare Company (RSC) stands as an enduring symbol of theatrical brilliance, firmly ingrained within the global cultural landscape.

Hollywood Comes Calling

The trajectory of Judi Dench's career, spanning from the realm of theatre to the illustrious world of Hollywood, is undeniably awe-inspiring. Her remarkable talent has firmly established her as a revered actress, capable of delivering exceptional performances that captivate audiences, whether it be on the grand stage or the silver screen.

In 1964, she made her highly anticipated Hollywood debut in the renowned film "The Third Man," thus initiating a remarkable trajectory in her cinematic journey. Throughout the passage of time, Dame Judi Dench has adorned the cinematic realm with her exceptional aptitude, thereby etching an enduring impression upon the world of film.

Among her most indelible performances on the silver screen are the enchanting portrayal in "A Room with a View" (1985), the heartwarming depiction in "Mrs. Brown" (1997), the delectable character in "Chocolat" (2000), and the captivating interpretation in "Notes on a Scandal" (2006). Dench's every performance was met with resounding critical acclaim, as she skillfully breathed life into a multitude of diverse characters, amassing a devoted following of admirers.

The exceptional accomplishments she attained in the realm of film were duly recognized, resulting in a multitude of commendations and honours bestowed upon her. Among these accolades was the prestigious Academy Award for Best Supporting Actress, which she received for her unforgettable depiction of Queen Elizabeth I in the renowned film "Shakespeare in Love" (1998). The magnitude of her talent garnered additional acclaim when she was bestowed with a prestigious Tony Award for Best Actress in a Play. This remarkable achievement solidified her status as one of a select few actresses who have achieved the trifecta of winning an Academy Award, a Tony Award, and a Laurence Olivier Award for Best Actress.

Dame Judi Dench's illustrious filmography encompasses a wide array of genres, serving as a testament to her remarkable versatility as an actress. With effortless grace, she effortlessly transitions between captivating period dramas, delightful comedies, and gripping thrillers, leaving audiences enthralled by her sheer brilliance.

During the course of her illustrious Hollywood tenure, Dame Judi Dench had the esteemed opportunity to engage in artistic partnerships with a plethora of distinguished luminaries within the entertainment realm. Among these esteemed individuals were the likes of the incomparable Meryl Streep, the esteemed Ralph Fiennes, and the venerable Colin Firth. The fact that she can effortlessly hold her own among the most esteemed individuals in Hollywood is a testament to her exceptional talent and unwavering professionalism.

Despite achieving tremendous success in Hollywood, Dame Judi Dench's unwavering passion for the theatre continued to burn brightly. With unwavering dedication, she consistently adorned the stage, solidifying her esteemed position as one of the world's most revered and adored actresses.

Within her extensive filmography, she proudly showcases a multitude of remarkable works. Notable among these is the acclaimed film "Skyfall" (2012), in which she skillfully portrayed the beloved character of M. Additionally, her exceptional talent as an actress was brilliantly displayed in "Victoria & Abdul" (2017), a film that truly highlighted the breadth of her abilities.

Her extensive collection of accolades, which includes prestigious BAFTA Awards and illustrious Golden Globe Awards, serves to fortify her esteemed position as a true luminary in the realm of cinema.

The impact of Judi Dench on British cinema is truly unparalleled. With her remarkable versatility, unwavering dedication, and undeniable brilliance, she has ascended to the status of a genuine icon, serving as a profound source of inspiration for actors and actresses across the globe, urging them to pursue greatness with unwavering determination. The mere mention of her name evokes a profound sense of admiration for her unparalleled talent in the realm of acting, establishing a lasting imprint that will undoubtedly serve as a wellspring of inspiration for future generations.

Chapter 3: The Icon, A National Treasure

Judi Dench's remarkable career has elevated her status to that of a revered national treasure, garnering her steadfast admiration and respect from both audiences and colleagues alike. With a career that has endured for over six decades, her extraordinary trajectory in the entertainment industry has made an indelible impact on both British cinema and the international stage.

Dame Judi Dench, an esteemed and adored actress of great repute in the United Kingdom, has made indelible contributions to the realms of both theatre and film, thereby cementing her position as an iconic figure. The impressive array of accolades adorning her illustrious career, which encompasses an Academy Award, two BAFTA Awards, an Olivier Award, and a Tony Award, serves as a testament to her extraordinary aptitude and the profound influence she has exerted on the entertainment sphere.

The unparalleled versatility of Dame Judi Dench is truly remarkable. With an innate ability to captivate audiences in classical theatre productions and command the silver screen in Hollywood blockbusters, she effortlessly embodies a diverse array of characters with unparalleled brilliance. With her remarkable talent for infusing vitality into every character she portrays, regardless of the genre, she has garnered adoration from audiences spanning multiple generations.

In addition to her exceptional acting abilities, Dench has showcased her remarkable vocal aptitude through her work as a voice actress in various animated films and television productions. With her unique vocal timbre, she has imbued beloved characters with a profound sense of depth and an irresistible charm, thereby highlighting her remarkable range of talents.

Judi Dench's eminence as a revered figure of national importance transcends her remarkable artistic accomplishments. She has emerged as a global exemplar for women, demonstrating that unwavering determination, diligent effort, and unwavering commitment can serve as the catalysts for achieving extraordinary success, irrespective of an individual's origins. The trajectory of her life, from a modest upbringing to the distinguished title of Dame of the British

Empire, stands as a compelling testament to the indomitable force of perseverance and unwavering passion.

Dame Judi Dench, renowned for her remarkable career, has consistently captivated and motivated audiences, thereby establishing a lasting legacy that is destined to reverberate for future generations. The magnitude of her influence on British cinema, theatre, and the acting profession as a whole is incalculable.

Judi Dench, a veritable icon and esteemed national treasure, has made profound contributions to the realm of entertainment, leaving an enduring imprint. With her exceptional talent, profound wisdom, and unwavering grace, she serves as a constant source of inspiration for actors and actresses worldwide. Her name shall forever be intertwined with the concept of excellence, while her enduring legacy shall forever be engraved within the hearts of those fortunate enough to have borne witness to her extraordinary displays of talent. The illustrious trajectory of Judi Dench's career as an actress and her personal growth as an individual stand as a remarkable testament to the transformative power that can be harnessed through unwavering dedication, unwavering determination, and an inexhaustible ardour for her craft.

The momentous occasion of Judi Dench's triumph at the Academy Awards, where she emerged victorious as the recipient of the esteemed Best Supporting Actress accolade for her remarkable performance in the renowned film *Shakespeare in Love*, stands as a pivotal milestone that firmly established her as an indelible icon within the realm of cinema. At the age of 63, she achieved the remarkable feat of becoming the eldest actress in history to be bestowed with an Oscar in the category of supporting role, thereby shattering conventional boundaries and illuminating her extraordinary aptitude and adaptability.

In the film *Shakespeare in Love*Dame Judi Dench delivered a remarkable performance as the formidable and enigmatic Queen Elizabeth I, embodying her character with unparalleled dignity and grace. The actress's portrayal skillfully encapsulated the very essence of the renowned historical figure, infusing the character with a profound sense of depth and subtle intricacies. Her skill in seamlessly blending drama and comedy within her portrayal garnered acclaim from both critics and audiences. Through her performance, she masterfully crafted a depiction of Queen Elizabeth I that exuded both regality and relatability.

The attainment of the Academy Award served as a confirmation of Dench's remarkable aptitude and unwavering commitment to her artistic pursuit. The acknowledgment was a testament to her unrivalled contributions to the realm of acting and her indisputable influence on the field. Receiving the award served as a catalyst for her career, propelling her towards unprecedented success in the realm of Hollywood.

In the wake of her triumphant Oscar victory, Judi Dench's star continued to radiate with undiminished brilliance. She captivated audiences on the silver screen with her remarkable performances in a series of highly acclaimed films, such as the emotionally stirring drama *Mrs. Brown* (1997), the enchanting and captivating *Chocolat* (2000), and the gripping and suspenseful thriller *Notes on a Scandal* (2006). Every role she portrayed exhibited her exceptional range as an actress and solidified her position as a prominent figure in the entertainment industry.

Nevertheless, despite achieving great success in Hollywood, Dench's unwavering dedication to the theatre remained unscathed. She persisted in gracing the theatrical stage, enchanting audiences with her extraordinary stage presence and mesmerising performances. In 1999, her exceptional portrayal in *A Room with a View* earned her the prestigious Tony Award, a testament to her remarkable talent and unwavering dedication to her craft.

The Academy Award victory of Judi Dench was not merely a personal achievement, but rather a significant milestone for women within the entertainment industry. With her remarkable triumph at an age when opportunities for actresses of advanced years were frequently constrained, she fearlessly confronted age discrimination while simultaneously emphasising the enduring potency of skill and creativity. She has emerged as a shining symbol of inspiration, demonstrating that age poses no obstacle when it comes to attaining remarkable success in one's professional pursuits.

Renowned for her remarkable achievements in British cinema, Judi Dench has garnered widespread acclaim for her invaluable contributions to the arts, earning her a legendary status that transcends borders. She continues to be a cherished and esteemed individual, revered for her exceptional abilities, modesty, and elegance. The trajectory of her career, spanning from the theatrical realm to the illustrious realm of Hollywood stardom, has been punctuated by a multitude of prestigious accolades and esteemed awards. This remarkable journey stands as a testament to aspiring actors and actresses worldwide, underscoring the undeniable truth that a potent combination of innate talent and unwavering passion serves as the quintessential formula for etching an indelible legacy within the realm of entertainment.

A Role Model for Women

The remarkable trajectory of Judi Dench, from her modest beginnings to her status as a globally renowned actress, stands as a testament to her indomitable spirit, exceptional aptitude, and resolute resolve. She serves as an exemplary figure for women, embodying qualities that ignite inspiration and instil empowerment in individuals of every generation, urging them to relentlessly pursue their aspirations and shatter societal limitations.

The remarkable strength and unwavering independence of Dame Judi Dench radiate brilliantly throughout her illustrious life and extraordinary career. She has consistently defied the influence of societal norms and expectations, opting instead to pursue her own aspirations and fervors. In the face of formidable challenges such as entrenched sexism and ageism within the entertainment industry, she exhibited unwavering resolve and ascended to the pinnacle of success, thereby underscoring the indispensable role of determination and self-assurance in attaining extraordinary accomplishments.

The manifestation of her grace and elegance is apparent not solely in her on-screen and on-stage performances, but also in her demeanour and public presence. Dench emanates an aura of composure and elegance, exemplifying the harmonious coexistence of strength and grace.

In addition to her exceptional acting abilities, Dench's intellect and quick-wittedness contribute to her captivating and engaging persona. With her keen intellect and delightful wit, she possesses endearing qualities that have captivated fans across the globe. She personifies the notion that intelligence and wit should be esteemed and applauded, irrespective of one's gender.

Dench's unwavering passion for her work is evident in her consistently exceptional performances, which serve as a testament to her unwavering dedication to her craft. The unwavering dedication she exhibits in each of her endeavours serves as a poignant reminder that the combination of diligent effort and fervent enthusiasm is the quintessential formula for achieving triumph.

In spite of her remarkable accomplishments and the numerous accolades she has received, Dench maintains a humble and grounded demeanour. She consistently maintains a strong connection to her origins and possesses a remarkable ability to engage and connect with both her fans and aspiring artists. The grounded nature of her personality further elevates her status as a role model, showcasing the significance of authenticity and maintaining a strong connection with one's own humanity.

Furthermore, the remarkable journey of Judi Dench as a resilient survivor, who has encountered numerous personal challenges, serves to enhance her status as an exemplary role model. She has adeptly manoeuvred through challenging circumstances, demonstrating the indispensable qualities of resilience and unwavering determination in the midst of hardship.

Dench, a steadfast feminist and ardent champion of women's rights, utilises her influential platform to vocally address the pervasive issues of sexism and discrimination within the industry. She fulfils the role of a mentor, providing guidance and support to young women, igniting within them a sense of inspiration to actively pursue their passions and fearlessly advocate for their beliefs.

The remarkable life and illustrious career of Judi Dench stand as a shining symbol of hope and inspiration for women across the globe. She exemplifies the notion that success can be attained through diligent effort, innate ability, and unwavering determination, irrespective of an individual's upbringing or prevailing conditions. The enduring legacy she leaves behind will serve as a wellspring of inspiration for countless generations of women, empowering them to fearlessly shatter barriers, wholeheartedly embrace their individuality, and ascend to remarkable achievements within their respective domains.

Chapter 4: The Legacy, A Dame of the British Empire

The legacy of Judi Dench, as a Dame of the British Empire, stands as a testament to her profound artistic contributions and enduring influence on the cultural landscape of Britain. The year 1988 marked a significant milestone in her career, as she was bestowed with the prestigious title of DBE. This appointment held immense historical significance, as it made her the trailblazing actress to ever be recognized with this esteemed honour for her remarkable contributions to the world of theatre.

Over the course of her remarkable career, which has spanned more than six decades, Dench has consistently served as a source of inspiration for actors and actresses worldwide. With unwavering commitment to her artistry, remarkable adaptability, and a remarkable talent for breathing life into characters, she has indelibly shaped the landscape of the acting industry. She is regarded as a role model by numerous aspiring artists who admire her unwavering dedication and profound enthusiasm for the arts.

The contribution of Judi Dench to the realm of Shakespearean plays has proven to be truly transformative, as she has succeeded in rendering the works of the bard more accessible and appealing to a wide range of audiences. With her remarkable portrayals of iconic characters from Shakespeare's repertoire, she has infused these timeless tales with a renewed vitality, captivating both seasoned patrons of the theatre and those experiencing it for the first time. Dame Judi

Dench's invaluable contributions to the realm of classical theatre have undeniably elevated the prominence of the arts, thereby enhancing the cultural encounters of innumerable individuals.

Dame Judi Dench, a trailblazing figure in the arts, has played a pivotal role in propelling the portrayal of women within the industry forward. With her remarkable achievements and widespread acclaim, she has effectively shattered the metaphorical barriers that hindered the progress of women in the acting industry. Her journey serves as a beacon of hope and motivation for aspiring actresses, unequivocally proving that one's gender does not limit the potential for success. This remarkable individual's story exemplifies the power of talent and perseverance, transcending societal expectations and redefining the boundaries of achievement.

Furthermore, the remarkable trajectory of Dench's life, from a humble upbringing to attaining the esteemed title of Dame of the British Empire, serves as a testament to her unwavering resolve and indomitable spirit. Her narrative serves as a poignant reminder that individuals of all backgrounds possess the capacity to attain extraordinary heights by virtue of their unyielding dedication and resolute commitment to their chosen pursuit.

The legacy of Judi Dench transcends the prestigious honour of her DBE. Over the course of her illustrious career, she has been bestowed with a plethora of prestigious accolades, which notably include two BAFTA Awards, an Olivier

Award, and a Tony Award. The achievements she has attained serve as a testament to her exceptional talent and profound influence on the realm of arts.

Furthermore, her esteemed affiliation with the Order of the Companions of Honour, the most prestigious accolade bestowed upon civilians in the United Kingdom, serves to further cement her esteemed position as an esteemed and beloved icon within British society.

Judi Dench, an indisputable icon of British culture, has left an indelible mark that will undoubtedly endure for generations to come. She continues to serve as a source of inspiration, a paragon of virtue, and an emblem of unparalleled artistic prowess, serving as a poignant reminder that the relentless pursuit of our passions can yield extraordinary accomplishments, irrespective of our individual circumstances. With her profound influence on the arts and her pioneering efforts in breaking barriers for women within the industry, her extraordinary narrative is poised to perpetually engender inspiration and captivate audiences on a global scale.

The recipient of the esteemed Praemium Imperiale award

The year 2011 marked a momentous occasion in the remarkable career of Judi Dench, as she was bestowed with the esteemed Praemium Imperiale, a highly prestigious accolade. The prestigious accolade, bestowed by the esteemed Japan Art Association in Tokyo, is widely regarded as one of the most esteemed honours within the realm of the arts. It is exclusively awarded to artists who have demonstrated exceptional prowess and made significant contributions to their respective fields. Dench's accolades in the realm of theatre and film serve as a testament to her remarkable aptitude and profound influence on both the stage and the silver screen.

Dame Judi Dench, a highly accomplished actress endowed with a multitude of talents, has captivated audiences worldwide with her extraordinary performances in a plethora of renowned films and theatrical productions that have become emblematic of our era. With her remarkable talent for embodying a diverse range of characters, infused with depth and authenticity, she has garnered immense respect and admiration from both audiences and fellow artists.

Over the course of her extensive and illustrious professional journey, Dench has consistently garnered widespread respect and admiration within the arts community. With unwavering dedication to her craft, an unwavering commitment to excellence, and an unwavering passion for acting, she has served as a profound source of inspiration for countless generations of actors and actresses, igniting within them the desire to pursue their artistic aspirations.

By joining the esteemed company of past recipients of the prestigious Praemium Imperiale, including luminaries such as Ingmar Bergman, Akira Kurosawa, and Meryl Streep, Dench's recent accolade further cements her position as an unequivocal icon within the realms of both theatre and film. The roster of recipients comprises esteemed individuals who have profoundly influenced and enhanced the artistic realm through their unparalleled contributions.

The award stands as a testament to Dench's exceptional talent, her steadfast dedication, and her noteworthy contribution to the arts. It stands as a poignant testament to her extraordinary accomplishments and enduring influence on the realm of entertainment.

The acknowledgement bestowed upon Judi Dench by the esteemed Praemium Imperiale is a thoroughly merited tribute to an actress whose profound impact on the realm of arts is undeniable. The enduring legacy of her work will serve as a timeless source of inspiration and delight, captivating and enriching audiences for generations to come.

She is a beacon of inspiration for all of us.

The remarkable journey and extraordinary achievements of Judi Dench stand as a profound source of inspiration for individuals hailing from diverse backgrounds. With her exceptional attributes and resolute resolve, she serves as a wellspring of inspiration and drive for individuals grappling with obstacles in their personal journeys. The following are several pivotal elements that contribute to the remarkable legacy she has left behind:

1. **Strength and Independence: Dench's** unwavering determination and rejection of societal conventions exemplify the profound influence of self-assurance and autonomy. She has steadfastly pursued her own unique journey, surmounting challenges with unwavering bravery

and resolute determination. Her remarkable resilience serves as a poignant testament, urging us all to remain steadfast in our authenticity and unwavering commitment to our own paths.

2. Graceful and Elegant: The poise and dignity exhibited by Dench, both in her personal life and public engagements, serve as a remarkable illustration of the significance of conducting oneself with grace and elegance. The display of her confidence and self-assuredness serves as a testament to the notion that it is indeed possible to exude elegance while staying true to oneself.

3. **Displaying Acute Intellect and Cleverness**: The sharp wit and quick humour exhibited by Dench serve to underscore the significance of embracing intelligence and cleverness. The demonstration of her capacity to connect with

individuals through her cleverness serves as a testament to the potency of a sharp intellect and a discerning sense of humour.

Passion is a driving force that fuels one's dedication and commitment to their work. In the case of this individual, she exudes an unwavering passion for her chosen profession. Her fervour is evident in every aspect of her work, from the meticulous attention The unwavering commitment Dench exhibits towards her craft is unmistakably apparent through the fervour she imbues into every single one of her performances. The unwavering dedication she exhibits in delivering her utmost effort serves as a poignant reminder to pursue our own passions with unwavering zeal and fervour.

One notable characteristic of this individual is their humble and down-to-earth nature. In spite of her widespread acclaim and achievements, Dench continues to exude an approachability and groundedness that sets her apart. The individual's display of humility offers a valuable lesson on the significance of maintaining a grounded perspective and preserving one's authentic identity.

Furthermore, Dench's remarkable resilience in the face of adversity, coupled with her unwavering commitment to championing women's rights, serves as a testament to her exceptional strength as an influential role model for women. The individual's capacity to surmount obstacles and persist serves as an empowering testament, reminding us to never relinquish our dreams and aspirations.

Moreover, Dench's unwavering dedication to perceptual learning and receptiveness to novel encounters serve as a compelling catalyst for us all to wholeheartedly embrace our innate curiosity and persistently pursue knowledge throughout the entirety of our existence.

The demonstration of her kindness and compassion serves as a poignant reminder of the significance of offering assistance to others and serving as a steadfast pillar of support and solace for those who are in dire circumstances.

Judi Dench's remarkable journey serves as a profound source of inspiration, imparting invaluable life lessons that resonate deeply within us. Through her experiences, we are reminded of the significance of embracing our unique identities, nurturing our deepest passions, confronting adversities with unwavering determination, maintaining a sense of humility and empathy, and perpetually seeking knowledge. The enduring legacy of her remarkable talent as an actress and her influential role as a beacon of inspiration for women reverberates through the passage of time, deeply resonating with individuals from various generations. Her impact reaches far and wide, stirring emotions and igniting a sense of motivation within people across the globe, compelling them to ardently pursue their aspirations with unwavering resolve and elegance.

Conclusion : A Life Well Lived

The life of Judi Dench stands as a remarkable testament to the profound influence of perseverance, authenticity, and compassion. Throughout her remarkable journey, she has exemplified a myriad of qualities that not only resonate deeply but also offer invaluable life lessons for each and every one of us.

The pursuit of one's dreams, it is imperative to maintain an unwavering determination and resilience. The notion of never giving up on one's aspirations is a fundamental principle that holds true in the face of adversity. Dench's resolute determination in the face of adversity exemplifies the significance of steadfastly clinging to our aspirations and refusing to be deterred by setbacks in our pursuit of objectives. The unwavering resilience she displays serves as a poignant reminder to maintain unwavering focus and unwavering commitment, even in the face of an uncertain path.

Embracing Authenticity: The confidence and independence exhibited by Dench serve as a powerful testament to the importance of remaining authentic and embracing our individuality. The individual's steadfast refusal to adhere to societal norms serves as a powerful catalyst for embracing authenticity and genuineness within our own personal journeys.

One should wholeheartedly embrace the concept of lifelong learning. The unwavering enthusiasm displayed by Dench in his pursuit of knowledge and his willingness to embrace novel experiences serves as a testament to the profound significance of perpetual learning and personal development. The individual's unwavering commitment to embracing curiosity and pursuing knowledge throughout the entirety of her existence serves as a testament to the notion that age should never serve as an impediment to the broadening of our intellectual and experiential horizons.

Incorporating kindness and compassion into one's daily routine is a valuable practice that can greatly enhance personal well-being and foster positive relationships with others. By consciously choosing to act with kindness and empathy, individuals can create a more harmonious and supportive environment for themselves and The genuine kindness and willingness to assist others exhibited by Dench serve as a powerful testament to the importance of extending a helping hand and cultivating compassion towards those in our midst. The compassionate essence she embodies serves as a poignant testament to the profound influence that even the most modest gestures of benevolence can exert upon the lives of those around her.

Throughout her illustrious journey, Judi Dench has ascended to the pinnacle of success, serving as an awe-inspiring beacon of hope and empowerment for women worldwide. Her remarkable trajectory stands as a testament to the indomitable human spirit, unequivocally demonstrating that the pursuit of greatness knows no bounds, transcending the constraints of one's humble origins. The life she leads serves as a shining example of the immense influence that can be achieved through unwavering commitment, tireless effort, and an unwavering love for one's chosen pursuit. Dame Judi Dench's remarkable achievements in both the esteemed realms of theatre and film have undeniably forged an enduring legacy. Her unwavering dedication to her craft has served as a profound source of inspiration for countless aspiring actors and actresses across generations.

In her capacity as a role model, she exemplifies the notion that a life imbued with grace, dignity, and intelligence is not merely attainable, but also deeply satisfying. The impact of Dench's influence extends far beyond her artistic accomplishments, reaching into the realms of authenticity, resilience, and compassion. The reverberations of her influence extend beyond her captivating stage and screen performances, resonating deeply within the lives of all who have the privilege of crossing paths with her.

Judi Dench's life serves as a remarkable testament to the profound allure of living with unwavering passion, wholeheartedly embracing one's unique individuality, and tirelessly uplifting others through acts of genuine kindness and unwavering support. The enduring legacy she leaves behind will serve as an ongoing source of inspiration and empowerment for individuals worldwide, acting as a guiding light for those who aspire to live their lives to the utmost potential.

A Stellar Career

The remarkable career of Judi Dench has made an enduring impact on the realms of film and theatre. For more than sixty years, she has adorned both the theatrical platform and the cinematic realm with her extraordinary prowess, enthralling audiences across the globe. With an extensive repertoire of iconic films and plays, she has garnered a multitude of accolades, solidifying her status as a revered national treasure.

Dame Judi Dench embarked on her illustrious journey in the realm of performing arts, commencing with her inaugural foray into the world of theatre in the year 1957. From the very beginning, she demonstrated her remarkable versatility and exceptional skill, taking on a diverse array of highly regarded productions, with a particular emphasis on the works of the esteemed playwright, William Shakespeare. The actress's interpretations of legendary Shakespearean figures, including Ophelia in **Hamlet**, Goneril in **King Lear**, and Cleopatra in **Antony and Cleopatra**, were widely acclaimed for their exceptional artistry, as they imbued these celebrated characters with profound intricacies and subtleties.

During the 1970s, Dench made her foray into the world of cinema, thereby cementing her already stellar reputation as an extraordinary actress. With her notable performances in acclaimed films such as "A Room with a View," "Mrs. Brown," and "Chocolat," she has garnered extensive acclaim and recognition, solidifying her position as a formidable presence in the realm of cinema.

Dame Judi Dench reached a remarkable milestone in her illustrious career when she was bestowed with the prestigious Academy Award for Best Supporting Actress. This well-deserved recognition was a result of her exceptional portrayal of the iconic Queen Elizabeth I in the critically acclaimed film Shakespeare in Love (1998). The acquisition of this esteemed accolade cemented her position as one of the industry's most esteemed and gifted actresses, signifying a significant milestone in her already illustrious professional trajectory.

Despite the multitude of accomplishments she has garnered, Dame Judi Dench's unwavering dedication to her craft remains resolute. Over the course of her career, she has consistently embraced demanding roles, showcasing her versatility in both the realms of cinema and theatre. The actress's remarkable performances in highly successful films such as "Skyfall" and "Spectre" served as a testament to her exceptional ability to enthral audiences through her magnetic charisma and undeniable talent.

In addition to her remarkable artistic contributions, Judi Dench's influence reverberates as a profound source of inspiration for actors and actresses across the globe. The remarkable combination of grace, dignity, and intelligence displayed by her throughout her journey to achieve great success serves as a powerful testament to her unwavering resilience and unwavering dedication. The life journey of Dench, characterised by triumphing over obstacles and embracing one's true identity, stands as an inspiring symbol of hope and empowerment for individuals from diverse walks of life.

The indelible mark of Judi Dench's legacy is firmly inscribed within the annals of British cinema and theatre. The mesmerising nature of her performances, whether in film or on the theatrical stage, will undoubtedly leave a lasting impact on audiences for many generations to follow. With her status as a genuine national treasure and an esteemed exemplar, she personifies the concept that excellence can be attained through innate ability, unwavering determination, and an unwavering devotion to one's chosen vocation.

The individual in question is undeniably a true icon.

The esteemed Judi Dench undeniably holds the well-deserved status of a true icon within the realm of British cinema. With an exceptional talent and an illustrious career that spans over six decades, she has firmly established herself as one of the most respected and beloved actresses worldwide. With a plethora of notable accolades to her name, encompassing an esteemed Academy Award, a distinguished Tony Award, and a coveted BAFTA Award, she undeniably demonstrates an extraordinary level of talent and adaptability across the realms of both cinema and the stage.

Over the course of her illustrious career, Dench has consistently captivated audiences both on the silver screen and the theatrical stage with her exceptional performances, thereby etching an indelible imprint on the realm of entertainment.

With her portrayal of Miss Lilly in the cinematic masterpiece **A Room with a View** (1985), her remarkable embodiment of Queen Victoria in the acclaimed film **Mrs. Brown** (1997), and her captivating performance in the enchanting tale **Chocolat** (2000), this talented actress has consistently demonstrated her ability to infuse depth and authenticity into a diverse array of characters. Furthermore, her depiction of the character M in the renowned James Bond film series, particularly in the critically acclaimed **Skyfall** (2012), has garnered widespread acclaim from both viewers and reviewers alike.

Dench's artistic prowess extends beyond the realm of acting, encompassing various other creative domains. Additionally, she has demonstrated her remarkable prowess as a voice actress, employing her unique vocal abilities to bring to life renowned characters like Nala in the critically acclaimed film **The Lion King** (1994) and Old Deuteronomy in the recent adaptation of **Cats** (2019). In addition, her profound affection for classical music has prompted her to unveil numerous albums, thereby showcasing her remarkable adaptability and unwavering ardour for the realm of arts.

Dame Commander of the Order of the British Empire, Dench has been duly acknowledged for her remarkable contributions to the arts, a distinction that stands as one of the most esteemed accolades within the United Kingdom. With a reach that transcends borders, her impact resonates not only within her homeland but also on a global scale, where she is revered as a beacon of inspiration for actors and actresses worldwide. With an unwavering commitment to her craft, coupled with her remarkable strength, independence, and grace, she emerges as an exemplary role model for women spanning across generations.

Judi Dench's iconic stature is further enhanced by her remarkable capacity to inspire and uplift multiple generations of artists. With an extraordinary trajectory that transcends modest origins and culminates in global acclaim, her remarkable odyssey stands as a luminous symbol of inspiration and unwavering resolve for burgeoning thespians. Throughout her illustrious career, she has consistently inspired and motivated countless individuals to wholeheartedly embrace their profound passion for the arts, urging them to persist and triumph over any obstacles that may come their way.

In summary, Judi Dench's status as a genuine British cinema icon is firmly established due to her extraordinary talent, extensive and illustrious career, and unwavering dedication to her artistry. She remains widely acclaimed for her exceptional acting talent, revered as a prominent figure within the arts community, and serves as a profound source of inspiration for artists and women across the globe. Undoubtedly, the enduring influence of her legacy will continue to radiate for years to come, leaving an indelible imprint on the realm of entertainment and serving as a wellspring of inspiration for countless generations of aspiring artists who aspire to emulate her remarkable journey.

Bonus content

Interviewer: Dame Judi, thank you so much for taking the time to speak with me today. I'm a huge fan of your work, and I'm honoured to have this opportunity to talk to you.

Judi Dench: It's my pleasure. Thank you for having me.

Interviewer: You've had an incredible career that has spanned over six decades. What are some of the highlights of your career?

Judi Dench: There have been so many wonderful moments throughout my career that it's difficult to single out just a few. However, some roles hold a special place in my heart. Playing Queen Elizabeth I in "Shakespeare in Love" was a tremendous honour and a role I truly cherished. "Mrs. Brown" was another significant film for me, and portraying M in the James Bond films allowed me to be part of such an iconic franchise.

But beyond individual roles, I've been incredibly fortunate to work with some of the most talented actors, directors, and artists, both on stage and on screen. Collaborating with such brilliant minds has been a continuous highlight of my career.

Interviewer: You're known for your versatility as an actress. You've starred in everything from Shakespeare to Hollywood blockbusters. What do you enjoy most about playing different roles?

Judi Dench: The joy of being an actor lies in the endless exploration of various characters. Each role presents unique challenges and opportunities for growth. It's like stepping into different worlds and experiencing life from various perspectives.

I relish the diversity of characters and genres because it allows me to constantly learn and develop as an artist. Whether it's a powerful Shakespearean queen or a modern-day spy chief, each role provides a chance to understand and empathise with different facets of human nature.

Interviewer: You're a role model for many actors and actresses. What advice would you give to young actors who are just starting out?

Judi Dench: My advice would be to stay true to yourself and your passion for the craft. Embrace your uniqueness and never compare yourself to others. Each actor's journey is different, and what matters most is your dedication to the art and your willingness to keep learning and growing.

Rejection is a part of this profession, but don't let it discourage you. Embrace every opportunity to perform, whether it's on stage or in small productions. Each experience will contribute to your growth as an actor.

Above all, stay humble and open to collaboration with others. Cherish the joy of acting and the power it has to connect with audiences on a profound level.

Interviewer: You're also a strong advocate for women's rights. What are some of the challenges that women still face in the entertainment industry?

Judi Dench: The entertainment industry has come a long way in terms of gender equality, but there are still significant challenges that women face. Women are still underrepresented in leadership positions, both behind the camera and in production roles. This lack of representation impacts the stories we see on screen and the perspectives we are exposed to.

Pay disparity remains an issue, with women often earning less than their male counterparts for similar work. Additionally, the industry has historically perpetuate ageism for women, which can limit opportunities for older actresses.

But I'm optimistic that positive changes are happening. More women are stepping into leadership roles, and their voices are being heard. The industry is gradually recognizing the value and importance of diverse storytelling, which includes stories by and about women.

Interviewer: Thank you so much for your time, Dame Judi. It was an honour to speak with you.

Judi Dench: The pleasure was mine. Thank you for your thoughtful questions.

Filmography

Judi Dench's filmography is nothing short of remarkable, with a wide range of roles that showcase her versatility and talent. Her journey in the theatre began with notable performances in iconic Shakespearean plays such as "Hamlet," "King Lear," and "Antony and Cleopatra." Over the years, she continued to excel in stage productions, including "A Room with a View,"

"The Importance of Being Earnest," and "The Cherry Orchard."

Transitioning to the big screen, Dench's film career flourished, earning her acclaim and recognition. Her roles in films like "Mrs. Brown," "Chocolat," and "Skyfall" demonstrated her ability to bring depth and authenticity to her characters. Her portrayal of Queen Elizabeth I in "Shakespeare in Love" earned her an Academy Award for Best Supporting Actress, solidifying her position as one of the finest actresses of her generation.

Beyond theatre and film, Dench has also contributed her voice to animated films like "The Lion King" and "Cats," showcasing her versatility as a voice actress. Additionally, she has taken on various television roles, including the popular series "As Time Goes By" and "Cranford."

Her achievements have been acknowledged with numerous accolades, including two BAFTA Awards, a Tony Award, and an Olivier Award, among others. Her appointment as Dame Commander of the Order of the British Empire in 1988 recognized her significant contributions to the arts and culture.

Notably, Dench made history as the oldest actress to portray M in the James Bond films, adding another iconic role to her already impressive repertoire. Moreover, she remains the oldest actress to win an Academy Award, showcasing her enduring talent and dedication to her craft.

Throughout her career, Judi Dench has continually broken barriers and challenged stereotypes, proving that age and gender are no limitations to achieving greatness in the entertainment industry. She is an inspiration to aspiring actors and actresses, demonstrating the power of perseverance, talent, and a passion for the arts.

With a legacy that spans over six decades, Judi Dench has undoubtedly left an indelible mark on the world of entertainment. Her talent, grace, and intelligence have made her a true icon of British cinema, and her contributions will continue to inspire and resonate with audiences for generations to come.

Printed in Great Britain
by Amazon

36829448R00066